MW00424347

WHAT'S YOUR
PLAN B?

Why You Would Be Brain Dead
Not to Own a Home-based Business

WHAT'S YOUR PLAN B?

*Why You Would Be Brain Dead
Not to Own a Home-based Business*

COURTNEY EPPS
ROBERT A. MCFADDEN

Clovercroft Publishing

What's Your Plan B?

©2020 by Courtney Epps and Robert A. McFadden

All rights reserved. No part of this book may be reproduced or
transmitted in any form or by any means, electronic or mechanical,
including photocopying, recording or by any information storage
and retrieval system, without permission in writing from the
copyright owner.

Published by Clovercroft Publishing, Franklin, Tennessee

Edited, cover designed, and interior designed
by Adept Content Solutions

Printed in the United States of America

ISBN: 978-1-950892-71-6

CONTENTS

PREFACE

Hi! We're Courtney Epps and Robert A. McFadden, co-authors of the book *More Relaxing Less Taxing for Network Marketers*. We're passionate about helping people achieve financial stability and time flexibility so that they can truly live the lives they want. Whether you desire more time with your family, more money to pay off debts or take vacations, or just the ability to strike a better work/life balance, you might find that you're currently unsatisfied with your financial situation. That's why we co-wrote this book, *What's Your Plan B?*

Have you ever felt like you're stuck in a rat race? Like your daily grind is taking up all of your time and energy but isn't giving you the results, you want? Our goal is to empower you by giving you a different way forward with your career. There are ways to get creative with how you make your money, and how to *keep* more of your money, and we're going to share them with you. And don't worry—this solution isn't about quitting your job and totally upending your life. It's about building a completely manageable side hustle that supplements your life and saves you money!

Courtney is a tax strategist and international speaker with over 19 years of experience helping people save money on taxes. Robert is a serial entrepreneur with over 27 years' experience starting companies, speaking internationally, and coaching network marketers to achieve their financial goals. Between the two of us, we have a wealth of knowledge and industry secrets about how to find meaning in your work and how to save money while you're doing it.

Not many people think to have a Plan B for their income. We were trained to get one job, show up every day without asking questions, and enjoy our lives when we retire. We all know this vision we were sold doesn't actually work. That's why having a Plan B is one of the best long-term decisions you can make for your financial health—and by "Plan B," we mean a home-based business.

In this book, you will learn:

- what a home-based business is;
- why it's the path towards greater financial stability;
- how a home-based business can save you money;

- what tax deductions you can start taking on money you're already spending;
- the challenges business owners face, and how you can stay resilient;
- why network marketing is the least risky option for your home-based business;
- how to set up your home-based business;
- everything you need to know about audits;
- and more!

Our goal is to equip you not only with knowledge about the benefit of home-based businesses but to also give you the tools to get started. By the end of this book, you'll be prepared to put your Plan B into action, securing your future and your family's future and finally enjoying the financially stable life you always wanted.

CHAPTER 1

What Is Your Plan B?

Why you would be brain-dead
not to have one

The world is rapidly changing. What was once seen as stable is now unstable. What we thought we knew about employment doesn't fit into this new world. Twenty-seven million more people recently found themselves without a job and still need to provide for their families. Business owners with tens of thousands of monthly overhead in rent, utilities, and payroll have been forced to close their businesses, maybe never to open their doors again. Some have put years, even decades, of blood, sweat, and tears into something that is being jeopardized daily by forces outside their control.

For many people, their Plan A for work and life doesn't work anymore. So the question is, What's your Plan B?

There is hope for your future. There is a way to find a path that is in your control, that is flexible enough to remain resilient in a changing world and that, for some people, can offer the financial safety and support they need.

By Plan B, we mean a home-based business. A home-based business is just what it sounds like: a business you operate out of your home, often through your computer. With no retail stores open, no malls, home-based businesses are exploding in sales. Instead of depending on a brick-and-mortar location or an office, income is flowing to businesses operating through technology. If anything, home-based businesses are doing better now than ever before.

Home-Based Businesses–by the Numbers

We're passionate about helping people keep their hard-earned money. You spend more hours away from your family than with them to be able to provide the best life you can. You pay a steep price for education, for living expenses, and to feel like you can enjoy your life in addition to covering the bases. But that cost of living takes an additional slice out of our income.

One of the realities of being Americans is we pay taxes. But have you ever wondered what your options are to pay *less* taxes, all while operating a business that offers you a more predictable future?

Did you know that the average household income in America is $61K? That same household will pay on average $12K in taxes, which leaves them with only $49K. The problem with this is that the average yearly cost of living in America is $53K. Let's do the math on these statistics. That means that the average person is working

40 hours a week, 50 weeks a year, to take two weeks' vacation, all while going into debt an average of $4,000 per year. Hence the reason why people are so far into credit card debt and student loan debt. The national debt in our country is more than $74,000 per citizen. That's startling!

We're going to share with you how you can fix these statistics by having a Plan B—a home-based business. Home-based businesses can take many shapes and forms, some with greater risk and others with less. The best way to approach starting a home-based business is to know your options and choose the least risky as a side hustle to supplement and diversify your income. As Warren Buffett said, "Never depend on one income. Make an investment to create a second source." We'll get into all the specifics, but first, let's explore the financial benefits of a home-based business so that you aren't among the many Americans accruing $4K in debt every year.

> *Warren Buffett said, "Never depend on one income. Make an investment to create a second source."*

The Two Tax Systems in Our Country

There are two tax systems in this country. One was created to take your wealth and fund the federal government.

Coincidentally, that first tax system is designed to keep you broke. That system is called the W2, or salaried employee system. This is the system that most Americans find themselves in, and until now, we were taught that this was the safest system to be in. We were taught to go to school, get good grades, and then get a good job.

What does that even mean? It means that you trade your time for dollars. Working for an entire lifetime can, and should, produce enough to secure your future. However, for individuals in the first tax system, this rarely happens. They end up in debt, working much longer than they expected, and sometimes passing their financial burdens onto their children. The salaried employee system makes promises it can't keep. It prevents us from truly enjoying the lives we were given. However, there is another option.

The true path to the life you imagined for yourself is through the second tax system, which is for business owners. That system was created to provide you wealth and allows you to keep it.

The business owner system is the backbone of the economy. Business owners create the first system—they provide jobs, and they need salaried employees to keep the system going. Someone must pay taxes to the government, and the salaried employee receives the lion's share of the tax burden. You may see this as unfair, but you must realize that if business owners did not get tax deductions, they would not be generating the millions of jobs that are needed for this country to continue. Seventy percent of job growth in our country was created from small businesses. Businesses are given more opportunities to claim deductions and expenses, aka less taxes, because a strong business is good for the economy as a whole, including the government.

However, the system is broken for salaried employees, and what's happening now should be a huge wake-up call for America. Did you know that before the COVID-19 virus pandemic, 46 percent of Americans did not have an extra $400 to their name, and 69% of Americans did not have an extra $1000? To make matters worse, 48% of US families headed by someone 55 or older have zero retirement savings. How are people supposed to get ahead—or even retire—if they're living paycheck to paycheck?

So, where is all the money going? Well, on average, 40 percent of the salaried employees' income is going to pay for taxes. It is likely that, as an employee, you will pay more in taxes throughout your life than you will on food, clothing, transportation, and housing combined! Add it up. Property taxes, Social Security taxes, federal, city, and state income taxes, license, sales tax, capital gains tax, use tax, the list goes on. How do we get past all of these taxes?

The Aha Moment: Courtney's Wake-Up Call

As an accountant of 19 years, I have had the privilege of working with small- to medium-sized businesses, as well as W-2 employees. I had a massive accounting and insurance agency, with 3,500 clients, by the time I was 29 years old. I put that business up for sale using an installment agreement, and four months later, the new owner stopped paying me. Because I had a five-year noncompete in the entire state, no money, and $8,000 a month in debt, I found myself in a tough spot. And yet, this is also when everything changed.

My parents happened to get me involved in a network marketing company, and someone I met asked if I would prepare their tax return, as it was their first year in network marketing. Although they had not made a lot of money, they had attempted to earn an income on a weekly basis with their home-based business.

I prepared their return, and they received $4,100 more than they had ever received before in taxes. This was my aha moment. Network marketing helps people find something they're passionate about and then gives them the opportunity to build a home-based business by sharing that product or service with others. And as for my role, I could help people save money while doing something they loved.

I started preparing taxes for hundreds of network marketers. After preparing more than 900 tax returns, I concluded that I could save the average person $4,000 to $8,000 in taxes by having a home-based business.

This new approach changed my perception about our tax system entirely. I was taught in school that network marketing or home-based businesses were not legitimate businesses, but I can tell you that is far from the truth. Network marketing and home-based businesses are the *essential key* to thriving inside our tax system and living the life you really want. Let me give you an example: Alexis is a W2 employee and has household bills (cell phone, mortgage or rent, utilities, car expenses, medical expenses, meals, and other miscellaneous expenses). She has to pay for all of these expenses using the money she has left over after she pays her taxes, what we call "after-tax dollars." If Alexis started her own business, some of the money she is already spending would be considered business expenses and become deductible from her ordinary taxable income.

Network marketing and home-based businesses are the essential key to thriving inside our tax system and living the life you really want.

There are tons of expenses that you are entitled to take when you have a home-based business, including travel, continuing education, hiring your kids, and your home office.

Alexis's home-based business allows her to keep more of her hard-earned money, in multiple ways. The government allows you to use your losses against any form of income, or you can carry those losses forward, forever. If Alexis earns $60,000 per year as a W2 employee and she generates a loss of $15,000 for her business, she would only pay taxes on $45,000. You will always pay less taxes as a business owner than a W2 employee. As a W2 employee, you make your money, pay taxes, and then hopefully buy your needs and some of your wants.

As a business owner, you can truly make money in your business, have business expenses (that are redirected from living expense—aka, wants and needs), and then pay taxes. That is the power of the wealth system.

How Do Wealthy People Think?

Financial independence is a big deal, and that is why people are willing to work, underpaid, for thirty years of their life. They think their pension—which are now almost extinct—and 401(k) are going to get them through their retirement. The sad truth is that most people will outlive the money they have set aside, not because they planned to fail, but because they failed to plan. They were not taught financial freedom in school, and they leave their money to be managed by people who don't even know them (these are commonly called fund managers). Wealthy people realize that 401(k)s, jobs, CDs, and IRAs are not going to make them wealthy. They work on another level. Their first principle is to pay the legal minimum in taxes. You must understand this: wealthy people have figured out ways to make more money through leveraging other people's time and/or money—all while paying less in taxes.

This book will show you how to pay less in taxes so you can be on a road to financial freedom. But you must first take the leap of faith and become an entrepreneur through your home-based business. We're not telling you to quit your day job. We're telling you to find something about which you're passionate and start a part-time business so that you can achieve the greatest tax savings possible.

What Must You Do in Order to Have a Home-Based Business?

You might be feeling excited about the prospect of a home-based business and all that it can do for you, but you also might have some questions. For example, if your home-based business is a side hustle, how many hours do you have to put toward it, especially if you have another job? Fortunately, the bar is fairly flexible. There are no hourly requirements for owning a home-based business. If you are willing to spend forty-five minutes, three to five days a week doing money-making activities, then you are entitled to deductions for a business.

> *There are no hourly requirements for owning a home-based business.*

You can work on your home-based business part-time or full-time. You do not have to make a certain amount of income to qualify as a home-based business. However, you must attempt to make an income, and you must run your business as if it were a legitimate business, not a hobby.

CHAPTER 2

Why Own a
Home-Based Business?

In addition to the financial argument, there are other reasons why you would want to own a home-based business. For example, there is a huge amount of pride in building your own dreams instead of someone else's; pride in building toward your goals of retirement, vacations, or a dream home; pride in being able to say, "I did this!" There's even a level of pride that your spouse, children, family, and friends carry. They will see your example of someone going after what they want in life, and they too will be changed by that.

We'd like to share some of the other powerful benefits of owning a home-based business.

The Benefits of a Home-Based Business

NO COMMUTE – We don't know about you, but sitting in traffic is like being locked in a room. Your freedom is stripped from you for that period of time. You're on lockdown. There's nothing worse than a long, congested commute that keeps you from your family and your opportunity to build toward your dreams. Owning a home-based business doesn't mean you'll never leave the house; it just means that you're able to eliminate the commute out of your life. You can choose to leave the house when traffic patterns work in your favor or when store lines will be short. Working from home increases your quality of living almost instantly. Even if you are stuck commuting for another job,

Working from home increases your quality of living almost instantly.

you can use that time to build toward your home-based business by listening to books on tape or networking with people through calls. Just because you have to endure a commute doesn't mean it has to be wasted time.

TAX DEDUCTIONS – This will get covered in greater detail as you read on, but come on people, there is so much to be said about the massive tax savings to be had by running a business out of your home! Even if you own a traditional business, run another business from your home. You get all sorts of deductions for making this simple financial decision. You get to write off a portion of your rent or mortgage, insurance, utilities, internet, phone, activities, amenities, and more. You'd be brain-dead *not* to run a business out of your home, if even for the deductions alone.

> *You get to write off a portion of your rent or mortgage, insurance, utilities, internet, phone, activities, amenities, and more.*

COST SAVINGS – Tax deductions aside, we really do put these two things in separate buckets altogether. Think about how much money you'll save on gas, wear-n-tear on your vehicle, additional rent/lease payments for an off-site location, and additional insurance and utilities. These reductions in SG&A expenses mean you can more competitively price your products or services, which makes you more flexible and nimble in the market. Adaptability will win the race more often than not. That flexibility brings us to number four.

ADAPTABILITY – As we've discussed, the world is ever changing, and it has recently shown us just how much it can change. Markets change. Consumer trends change. Owning a small home-based business will allow you the flexibility and adaptability to quickly pivot your messaging without an insane blow to your overhead. Home-based businesses are easy to refine and hone to fit the current world dynamics. Conserve your cash until you have nailed your value proposition, and then run hard!

Home-based businesses are easy to refine and hone to fit the current world dynamics.

TIME FLEXIBILITY – Individuals who take the leap into entrepreneurship through a home-based business are often after two things: financial stability and time flexibility. Notice we didn't say financial freedom. Financial freedom is so far removed for the majority of Americans that it's defeating to set a target that seems unachievable so early on in one's business journey. The concept that you can make so much money that your money now works for you does not compute in the average 9–5 mindset. But if we're talking about financial stability, now that's something we can reach! The average Bob and Barbara in America can see themselves with enough extra cash from their side-hustle business to give them greater stability. Once that goal is reached, then it's time to dream bigger and shoot for the next rung on the ladder of success. Time freedom works almost the same way. The idea that someone has *no demands* on their time seems unrealistic and unachievable. What is achievable is a flexible schedule that can allow us to meet our kids at the bus stop with a smile or get in a workout when it suits us best. Time flexibility is one of the best possible advantages to running a home-based business. Never missing a sporting event or a dance recital is one of the things for which we're most grateful. When your work schedule is 100 percent at your discretion, you can plan your hours around important personal activities throughout the day—a priceless boon.

Time flexibility is one of the best possible advantages to running a home-based business.

BUILDING A BRAND AND EXPERTISE – Building a brand for your business is not only fun, it gives you another level of satisfaction—that you have created something bigger than yourself. Also, as you develop your business and your brand, your expertise in that field continues to increase, allowing you to not only make more money but also providing you opportunities to speak and get paid to share what you know in your industry. The more you learn in business, the more you earn.

The more you learn in business, the more you earn.

JOB SECURITY – Job security is drastically declining. Every day, millennials are replacing baby boomers in jobs. With the advent of massive technology, the things we went to school for are becoming more obsolete—and this could leave you without a job. People are being replaced with computers and other forms of AI. Many of us fear we will one day lose our job, and we won't be able to train in a new area of employment. By owning your business, you learn a valuable set of skills, and honestly, these skills will see you through anything. Even if one business fails, you

By owning your business, you learn a valuable set of skills, and honestly, these skills will see you through anything.

can start another, and you won't be starting from square one. Knowing the basics of how to run your own business is the most versatile skillset you can have.

PURPOSE AND GIVING – For a lot of us, our work doesn't connect us to a feeling of purpose or fulfillment. Whether through time or money, giving back to your community not only makes you feel good, it can become

Whether through time or money, giving back to your community not only makes you feel good, it can become a valuable part of your business.

a valuable part of your business. We'll talk more about this in the last chapter, with personal examples, but for now know that giving feels great *and* you can save tax dollars at the same time!

ALWAYS EXCITING – Another great thing about running your own business is that things are constantly changing. Sometimes they change for the worse and sometimes for the better, but you can never say that running your own business is boring. It is more like a roller coaster ride. Working for someone and doing the same thing over and over again makes for a very boring life. When running your home-based business, you'll meet multitudes through your clients and networking, and you'll find that many of them become like-minded friends. The system of relationships starts to feed on itself, making referrals to your growing network and receiving them, too. Even better, you can create your own mastermind groups and get feedback on your business. When you face a crisis or things are not going as planned, you have people you can reach out to, who can help you through the bad times, because they understand the bad

You can create your own mastermind groups and get feedback on your business.

times only stay for a little while. Your business community becomes a new family of sorts, and you'll wonder how you ever made it without them.

CONTINUING EDUCATION – The need for continuing education in business is crucial, and there is a plethora of amazing leaders from whom you can learn (and write off your education as tax deductible!). Some of the people we like to follow are Tony Robbins, Les Brown, Steve Harvey, Jim Rohn, Zig Ziglar, John Maxwell, Eric Worre, and Grant Cardone. All of these people are like our mentors; we still rely on the things we've learned from them through events, videos, and books. Here's one golden nugget Courtney learned in her continuing education that made a huge difference in her life: you are the average of the top five people you spend time with. If you are the most successful person in your group, you may want to find another group of people to hang out with or choose to go to some events to spend time with people who can help you grow as a person and business owner. Each continuing education event we attend sets us on a new, reinvigorated path. It helps us get better every day, and our businesses have grown exponentially from the information we've learned from other leaders.

Each continuing education event we attend sets us on a new, reinvigorated path.

NO SUCH THING AS FAILURE – It's true that when you start your own business, there are things you don't know—and you often don't know until you know! Much of the business journey is a series of experiments, trial and error, and learning as you go. The secret is you really can't fail—not if you keep going. Some mistakes cost time, and others cost money, but don't be ashamed by them. Take each lesson and hold it close to your heart as a reminder of what you gained and how it helped you move your business to the next level. Sometimes you have

Take each lesson and hold it close to your heart as a reminder of what you gained and how it helped you move your business to the next level.

to jump in feet first and learn as you go. And if you allow it, your failures will become your biggest lessons.

MENTORSHIP – As you gain experience in your home-based business, you'll find that your knowledge and experience are invaluable to others. Like giving, mentoring is a great way to give back and to feel a sense

Like giving, mentoring is a great way to give back and to feel a sense of purpose.

of purpose. There's nothing more rewarding than taking someone under your wing and sharing valuable skills they can use to make their life better.

REINVENT YOURSELF – As you continue to get better at what you do in business, opportunities come your way that you would not have had access to otherwise. This allows, if you want, the chance to constantly transform or reinvent yourself to be and do what you want to do, not what you have to do. As an entrepreneur, you can be whatever you want—as opposed to, believe it

> *As an entrepreneur, you can be whatever you want.*

or not, being a doctor or lawyer. Also, you can start a new business or service tomorrow if you get bored with what you're doing, and it doesn't have to cost you a lot of money or years in education to do so.

CHANGING THE WORLD – You may say that every business owner thinks they are going to change the world, but that your service or business may not be life changing. Take a look at these people: Walt Disney, the Rockefellers, Sam Walton, Bill Gates, Steve Jobs, Tony Robbins. All had visions of what they wanted to do for themselves and their families. While they were building their businesses, they just so happened to inspire people, change the world as we know it, and carry a lot of people along the way. Eventually, each of these people ended up with less of a business and more of an empire! So, even if you think your idea is not a big deal, do not sell yourself short. We tend to overestimate what we can do in one year but drastically underestimate what we can do in five

20

to ten years. Start something now that is life changing for you, your family, and everyone surrounding you. Who knows what it will become?

We tend to overestimate what we can do in one year but drastically underestimate what we can do in five to ten years.

Truly, owning our own businesses was one of the best things that happened to us. And if these benefits are any indication, we know it will be one of the best things that happens to you, too.

Business owners see light at the end of a tunnel that no one else sees. The determination to continue when everything looks bleak is a great asset in business, and if you obtain that skill, it will affect every part of your life. We have both known the feeling of giving up too early. But then, in our own ways, we've learned that there are plenty of things worth finishing—such as this book, a diet and exercise plan, a better life for our families. Business forces you to realize that although times get hard, they will not stay that way. There is a season for everything, and business owners know all too well what that means. The determination to be a business owner has made us better spouses, parents, friends, and employers, because we realize you can't give up when things look bad. We have both failed and succeeded in business numerous times. We've had to pick ourselves up, dust ourselves off, and keep going for our families and everyone else who depended on us. That resilience is even worth more than what we save in tax dollars.

CHAPTER 3

Commonly Overlooked Challenges of Starting a Business

There is a great business case for starting a home-based business. From being able to deduct taxes on money you're already spending, to possibly reducing your taxable income from other work you might be doing. There is also a great psychological case—you have greater time flexibility; you can start working toward your dreams rather than someone else's; you can build something you're proud of; you'll create a network of fellow business owners who will support you and become lifelong friends.

Even though starting a business from the comfort of your own home has many benefits, there are some challenges. Our intention isn't to throw you into the deep end but to give you a realistic and optimistic view of what's possible.

Entrepreneurship is inherently risky, which is why it's smart to choose an entry point that is lower risk and requires very little overhead, such as network marketing (more on that later!).

To help you decide the best path forward for your home-based business, let's discuss some of the challenges many people overlook or downplay when starting a business.

Lack of Capital

A large number of small businesses fail each year. According to the Small Business Administration, of those that fail, 80 percent are from a lack of funding or working capital. In most cases, a business owner is very aware of how much money is needed to keep their business operating on a day-to-day basis, including funding payroll, paying overhead expenses such as rent and utilities, and ensuring their outside vendors are paid on time. However, sometimes owners don't fully understand how many sales they need to make to generate enough money to fund their expenses. This disconnect leads to funding shortfalls that can quickly put a small business out of business. Start with sufficient money to see your vision all the way through.

Start with sufficient money to see your vision all the way through.

Pricing

In addition to finding funds for working capital, many business owners miss the mark on pricing their products and services. To edge out the competition in highly saturated markets, new entrepreneurs often price their products or services too low. They view similar offerings in the market and price theirs lower with the intent to win customers over on price. While this strategy is successful in the short term, businesses end up closing their doors after keeping the price of a product or service too low for too long.

Lower prices are often used to entice customers to choose your service over your competitors', but once you have them, take care of them. Avoid the traditional business trap of getting them in the door through "new customer pricing" only to slowing jack up the prices over time. Instead, do some work to find the right balance between offering value you can stand behind and choosing a price that's sustainable for your business's longevity. It might take a bit of tweaking, but once you find that sweet spot for pricing, you'll notice that your business stabilizes.

The Lean Start-Up Phase

Starting a business on a budget is very possible, though not always easy. If you plan to succeed, then you will follow a process; if you can follow a process, then your success can be engineered; if it can be engineered, it can be trained. What this means is your success can be taught, even on a small budget. Don't get overwhelmed by not having enough cash or time to do everything you want to do. The important thing is determining and prioritizing the tasks that will result in the greatest outcomes. It's like being a ninja in selective reasoning. You will constantly ask yourself, "Is this really what I need to be doing to maximize my resources?" Or, "Is this going to get me the results I need faster than X?" Don't let overwhelm win. Keep a cool head, constantly assess your daily behaviors, and don't be afraid to leave some tasks on the table because they're just not the most important things right now.

Inadequate Management

Another common reason small businesses fail is because of a lack of business acumen. In some instances, a business owner is the only senior-level personnel within a company, especially when a business is in its first or second year of operation. While a business owner may have the skills necessary to create and sell a viable product or service, he or she often lacks the attributes of a strong manager and the time required to successfully manage other employees. Without a dedicated management team, a business owner has a greater risk of mismanaging certain aspects of the business, such as finances, hiring, or marketing.

Smart business owners outsource the activities they do not perform well or have little time to do successfully. A strong management team is one of the first additions a small business needs to make. Lacking a clear business plan and being unwilling to adapt plans as challenges arise can create problems for any small company.

Marketing Mishaps

A common blind spot for first-time business owners is how much money they'll need to invest in marketing.

When companies underestimate the total cost of early marketing campaigns, it is often difficult to redirect

Smart business owners outsource the activities they do not perform well or have little time to do successfully.

capital from other business departments to make up for the marketing shortfall. Because marketing is a crucial aspect of any early-stage business, it is necessary for companies to ensure they have established realistic budgets for current and future marketing needs. Similarly, having realistic projections in terms of target audience reach and sales conversions is critical to the success of any marketing campaign. Entrepreneurs who do not understand these tenants of sound marketing strategies are more likely to fail than companies that take the time to create and implement cost-effective, successful campaigns.

Did you know that a home-based business is started every 12 seconds in the US? Isn't that amazing? However, according to the Small Business Association, 80 percent of small businesses fail even though:

- they bring in revenues of more than $427 billion per year;

- 44% of home-based businesses are started for less than $5k; and
- 20% of home-based businesses make $100K-$500K a year.

Entrepreneurs who do not understand these tenants of sound marketing strategies are more likely to fail than companies that take the time to create and implement cost-effective, successful campaigns.

Even though we've have taken the time to outline some of the challenges to starting a home-based business, you should not be discouraged. There are a variety of different ways you can go about building a home-based business, and some of them have greater risk than others. For example, the majority of affiliate models and multi-level business opportunities help you avoid some of the challenges outlined above altogether. They require less initial capital, they have infrastructure to remove some of the management burdens, and they are incentivized to help you succeed.

As a distributor or representative of a network marketing company, you are responsible for selling products and services, and that's pretty much it. The company takes on the responsibility of product procurement, customer service, training, commissioning, branding, operations, technology, trips and incentives, and all sorts of other things. Your risk is essentially zero, and your only true responsibility as a business owner is to introduce new people to the products, services, and other opportunities your company offers. With minimal cost out of pocket and unlimited earning potential, shut the front door! That is A-MAZE-ING!

CHAPTER 4

Home-Based Business Options

Direct Sales, Affiliate Marketing, or Network Marketing

Just so we are working from the same page, when we refer to relationship marketing, network marketing, or direct sales, unless otherwise clarified, all three of these are interchangeable and we are talking about the same thing. Affiliate marketing is a bit different in that you can generate a side hustle income by selling other people's products and services while making a margin from the sales without assuming any of the risk or cost associated with creating that which you are selling. There are plenty of ways to generate a side-hustle income, from creating an online store on Amazon or selling your handcrafted good on Etsy, to driving Uber or delivering food for Grub-Hub. Technology keeps expanding the options, and it seems like there's something for everyone. Other options resemble a side "career," such as real estate investing, buying and flipping cars, starting a podcast, or consulting. People want goods and services, and if you create a side hustle to satisfy those needs, people will pay you for your efforts.

We have both explored several of these different options, though most were short lived. We have found that the option with the best staying power is a really good direct sales business or a relationship marketing company, also called "network marketing". These com-

> *We have found that the option with the best staying power is a really good direct sales business or a relationship marketing company, also called "network marketing".*

panies are reasonably priced and allow you to begin on a part-time basis. Plus, if you find one about which you're really passionate, it often doesn't even feel like work!

Direct sales has many benefits, including personal and business development, amazing relationships, and more clients. Courtney indirectly quadrupled her accounting practice thanks to network marketing! She works with numerous leaders in the industry, helping them do three things: attract, retain, and grow their customer base and teams. Robert has had equally great success with his coaching business through network marketing, helping thousands of people level-up their skills, increase their income, and climb the ranks in their companies.

Although the benefits of a network marketing company are vast, we need to make a disclaimer: please understand that you can't just sign up with a company and expect tax deductions; you have to attempt to earn an income. The best way to show the IRS you're making every effort is by sharing the company and products with your friends and family. A little-known secret is attending training events and subscribing to the tools offered for tax savings. Education is power, but it also lets the IRS know you are truly treating this as a business—and that you intend to make money. Let's explore this a bit further and how education in network marketing is a great way to grow as a person and get tax deductions.

Education and Network Marketing

Honestly, we could fill an entire book talking about the amazing aspects of network marketing. For brevity's sake, we'd like to focus on one benefit that also relates to a big deduction you can make on your taxes: ongoing education.

With network marketing, you don't have to know anything about entrepreneurship to get started. You don't need a certain degree, certain life experience, or anything. The reason is, there are innumerable tools, resources, and opportunities for education that you will be given through your network marketing company. They *want* you to succeed; and not just a nameless, faceless company—every single entrepreneur who's a part of that company is there to support and encourage you.

You don't need to have answers when you join network marketing, but you do need to be curious, teachable, and willing to learn. There are two primary ways in which you can invest in your education: one is through online courses and tools, and the other is through in-person

> *There are two primary ways in which you can invest in your education: one is through online courses and tools, and the other is through in-person events.*

events. The online courses are a great way to have a self-paced experience. You can learn from numerous different thought leaders—some of whom are really expensive to see in person—in the comfort of your own home. Some courses also have private communities you can be a part of in order to continue learning from this individual, which also provides you with the chance to connect with other like-minded individuals.

For example, we each have our own online courses and private communities where we check in weekly to address our community members' questions, provide relevant content, and support their expanding knowledge and expertise. As you could have guessed, Courtney's community is focused on cutting-edge tax strategies, while Rob's is high-level coaching in network marketing. Whether through online courses, books, or other tools that support your business mastery, you can deduct the cost of any education with a home-based business. Think about it like this: it's as if you're investing in another college degree, but you're saving money on your taxes, and you can actually personalize your education to fit your passions!

The other notable area of education investment is events. Every network marketing company has at least one large event every year. The intention is to bring all the entrepreneurs together, foster connection, ignite motivation, offer workshops, and sometimes unveil new products or services.

They say that every network marketing business is built from event to event. What this means is that each event is like an anchor of security you can drill into your business to create a greater foothold. You know how in rock climbing, when a climber is charting a new course, they drive anchors into the rock every six feet or so? It's a moving safety net. If they fall anywhere on their ascent, they'll only ever fall to their last anchor. They never fall all the way down to the ground.

Events are like those anchors. You never fall below your last anchor. There's a reason for this. Events are a chance for you to continue shaping your mindset and to deepen relationships with people who also possess that same mindset. People come into network marketing with different experiences and expectations of what's possible based on examples they've seen. For some, their friends in relationship marketing were really successful, and they believe they can be, too. For others, they only ever saw their friends struggle, and they're still a bit skeptical of what's possible for them. Events both equalize and elevate these mindsets. They cultivate everyone's belief that their dreams are possible, and not only that but that each person is surrounded by a safety net of their fellow entrepreneurs and the company as a whole. Each event lifts you up to that next anchor point, and you can trust that you'll never fall beneath it.

That's why events are so critical to anyone on a network marketing journey. They do more than educate you. They shape your mindset, continue to fill your tool belt, and connect you to a community of support and encouragement. And, of course, they're tax deductible—*and* they demonstrate that you are actually working on a legitimate business!

Network Marketing Reduces Risk

You already know some of the challenges of owning your own business. The risk can be very real, and we both have had instances where we experienced those risks firsthand. For example, Rob owned a retail store many years ago that was so successful, he opened multiple locations. However, after an unfortunate set of circumstances, he had to close his businesses. He was fortunate to keep his house, but it was a close call. This isn't to scare you but to be real with you. Owning a business, even a home-based business, is filled with unforeseen hurdles, and some options are safer than others.

Starting something completely on your own is the riskiest. Not only are you responsible for making sure that everything gets done in order to operate your business, you have to be all of the roles at once—CEO, marketer, sales representative, CFO, and so forth. This is why an option with less responsibility is so appealing, which is why a lot of people buy into a franchise. They have the company name and reputation, and that franchise will provide a lot of the structure for the individual's business. It's lower risk but can also be incredibly expensive. Successful franchises know what a valuable service they offer, and they charge through the roof for new entrepreneurs to sign on.

This is why we believe that network marketing is the least risky, most approachable, and most lucrative option for home-based business owners. Like a franchise, all of the work has been done for you. The brand is developed, the technology is managed, the support system is there. Each entrepreneur gets to put their name and face on top of a fully developed template, making their home-based business their own, without starting from scratch. And the risk is incredibly low! With a low entry fee, no warehouse of inventory to lose if things don't work out, no brick-and-mortar building that needs rent, no risk of losing your house—as far as entries into the home-based business world go, this is arguably the best one. Plus, if for some reasons you aren't satisfied with the company or product/service, you can easily step away and find a company that does fit. You remain flexible, have the opportunity to make an exponential income from other people in your network, and you're never truly on your own.

Now that we've explored some of the structural aspects of starting a home-based business, let's get into some of the nitty-gritty detail about how you actually save money through your taxes.

CHAPTER 5

Who Will Help You Save Money on Your Taxes?

(What you don't know is costing you thousands of dollars a year—or more!)
As taxes can take up as much as 50 percent of your income, tax planning is one of the most important investments you can make.

—Courtney Epps

By this point, we've demonstrated how powerful it is to have a home-based business. But even forming a home-based business isn't enough. You have to be aware of what it takes to actually prepare for your taxes and properly file, so that you don't end up paying more than you need to. It's critical that you educate yourself on the basics of the tax world, who's here to help you save money, and who you *think* is helping you to save money but might not be.

Through Courtney's years of work, she can verifiably say that most self-employed people, even when using a good accountant, overpay, on average, about $7,000 or more per year in taxes per $100,000 in sales. This is a *huge* amount of money for a small- to medium-sized businesses. If you add that up over ten or more years, it could be hundreds of thousands of dollars that could have been put back into your business, used to pay off a mortgage, placed in a retirement account, or used to pay for your kids' college tuition.

Every day we run into clients who are trying to cut costs with their businesses. The problem is they are cutting costs on some of the most important aspects of the business, things as marketing, payroll, and accounting, when they should be investing in tax planning and cost accounting so they can save on their biggest expense: taxes. Companies that are just getting started are often strapped for cash. These owners are trying to grow a business on a very small budget. Small companies tend to try to handle the accounting on their own and then hire an office manager/bookkeeper to handle the books later. The bad part about this is the owner usually has no time to check up on the work of the bookkeeper, and as long as the sales—and bills—are still coming in, no one is taking a close look at what is being done. We're not saying the bookkeeper is, in any way, failing to do his or her job, but we have found that what a business owner thinks a book-keeper is *supposed* to do and what that person actually *does* are usually two different things. Let's take a moment to look at the different roles you might encounter in the world of home-based businesses and taxes.

Bookkeeper

A bookkeeper's role is to input data and handle accounts payable and accounts receivable. This person is there to pay your bills and collect money from your clients. Thus, bookkeepers usually have no understanding of financial statements and what they need to do to help you save money.

Payroll Company

Some businesses hire a payroll company. Their job is only to make sure that your payroll is paid, that taxes are paid, and that payroll filings are taken care of.

Tax Accountant / CPA

Then there is the tax accountant or CPA. This is the person business owners put their faith and trust in. They hope their CPA will save them money, especially in taxes. What they don't understand is that the tax accountant is usually the person spending the least amount of time looking at the numbers. Also, by the time the accountant gets the information they need to prepare your return, the year is already up, and there is not much that can be done to save money on taxes.

Business Coach or Consultant

The business coach or consultant is like an intersection of information and planning. They're trying to help you run your company based on the numbers given to them by three different resources: the bookkeeper, tax accountant, and payroll company. But guess what the problem is? Although all of these people are talking to the business owner, they aren't talking to each other.

Fractional CFO

So how *do* you navigate the tax world for your business so that you're actually making choices throughout the year that will result in lower taxes? Who can plan the big picture with you, and who has your business's best interest at heart? If you want a clearer picture of your business, a fractional CFO is crucial, and this person will save you more money in your business than what he or she will cost. A fractional CFO is an experienced CFO you can hire part-time, or on retainer. They will work as your second brain, helping you make financial decisions that will actually result in the tax reductions you seek.

The sad truth is that out of all these roles, besides the fractional CFO, none are helping you save money in taxes, because that is not what you hired them to do—nor is it their expertise. In Courtney's five years of college, there was not a single class on "how to save your clients money." If there had been, she would have taken it! The classes offered dealt with how to prepare good books for tax preparation and how to prepare good financials to help with cost accounting.

Tax Preparation vs. Tax Planning

There are two different basic concepts you should know, called "tax preparation" and "tax planning." Tax preparation deals with income and numbers from the past. It is what has to be done to get the filing completed so you can get your tax returns finished. Meanwhile, tax planning determines ways to minimize the amount of taxes a client has to pay by thinking through future behaviors that will save money. Now, you may be saying to yourself that tax planning is not important because you didn't make a lot of money this year. This could not be further from the truth. Even if your deductions exceed your income, then you are able to take those losses, dollar for dollar, against any income you have. It serves to plan, even if you don't expect to make more money than you spend.

It serves to plan, even if you don't expect to make more money than you spend.

Example: Jim earned $75,000 in salary. His wife Sally is in a home-based business, and it generated a loss of $18,000. This loss would be deducted from Jim's salary, leaving them $57,000 net income on which to pay taxes. So what happens if you have more expenses than you do income in one year? The IRS allows something called a Net Operating Loss (NOL) carryforward, and it allows you to take the losses to deduct against any earnings in the future.

Example: Sally has a loss of $20,000 from her business from a previous year and $10,000 in losses this year. Jim and Sally would only pay taxes on $45,000 of Jim's $75,000 salary because of the carryforward. This would save more than $10,000 in taxes.

As you can see, tax planning strategy is hugely important regardless of how much money you make. In their great book *The Millionaire Next Door: The Surprising Secrets of America's Wealthy,* authors Thomas Stanley and William Danko analyzed multimillionaires and their mindsets. They discovered the rich believe that, in order to get rich, you have to get your taxes down to the legal minimum. In other words, you need to understand the rules of the tax game. The wealthy don't pay less in taxes because they are rich. They are rich because they pay less in taxes.

The authors show that most people who became millionaires were average people who saved money each year and invested that money for thirty or more years. Now, you may be saying to yourself that you do not have extra money to invest! That is why you must understand that tax planning is absolutely crucial and how it can allow you to keep more of your money so you can become wealthy one day as well.

Not All Accountants Are Made Equal

We're not saying accountants aren't important. Of course they are! It's just that people expect their accountant to be looking out for them in ways that they aren't. Part of the reason is your accountant often doesn't get your tax documents until January or February. That person then begins doing your taxes along with about two hundred to three hundred other returns! This leaves them roughly two to three hours to deal with your return. The other problem is that if the information is not getting to them until the new year, minimal tax planning strategies are going to be able to be used for the *previous* year. This is like saying that if you sign up for a gym membership, that alone will take care of your weight and health. The truth is, if you do not regularly utilize that membership, it does you no good. The same holds true for your taxes. If you are not utilizing a tax strategist outside of tax season for tax planning, it will cost you a lot more in taxes than you could ever pay for the service!

> *If you are not utilizing a tax strategist outside of tax season for tax planning, it will cost you a lot more in taxes than you could ever pay for the service!*

Another thing people take for granted is the individuality of accountants. Not all accountants are created equal. If you put ten different accountants in a room with the same tax information, you will typically come away with ten different tax returns. Why? Because it depends on the accountant's view of the tax code, their knowledge, and their experiences. If your accountant tells you that you can't write off a business expense because you have not made a profit, run! Why? Because almost all businesses have a loss for the first couple of years as the owner or owners are growing and funding the company with their own money. Such poor advice would be like telling Chrysler and Ford that they could not claim losses in 2008 and 2009 when almost every area of the auto industry similarly took a huge hit.

Here's a good principle: if a big business can make a deduction, a small business should be able to, too. If your accountant tells you that you should not write off certain things because it could trigger an audit, find another accountant. This person is not going to help you save money, and this advice will cost you an arm and a leg in the long run.

Of course, understand that you have to be in business for the main purpose of earning an income. You cannot just join a network marketing or home-based business company because you want tax write-offs, or to buy products at wholesale and just claim them as a business expense. The IRS states that a tax-deductible business expense is any expense that is incurred for the purpose of gaining or producing income with a reasonable expectation of future results. What does this mean? If you are attempting to earn an income, whether you do or not, you are deemed to be in business and therefore entitled to business deductions. Next, we will show you numerous tax deductions that aren't even taught to accountants in school. They have to be researched separately from books by other experts and from the IRS tax code, publications, and letter rulings. But once you know them, then you can start finding ways to pay the minimum amount of tax required.

CHAPTER 6

Commonly Missed Tax Deductions for Home-Based Businesses

Cutting back on taxes is the number-one move that will put more money in your pocket, and it is the fastest and easiest way to do so. Through this book, we want to stop you from giving away all of those extra hundreds and thousands of dollars and show you how you can get every deduction you are legally entitled to receive.

The first step is to look at deductions you are not currently using, or deductions that are slipping through the cracks. For example, Courtney recently amended three years' worth of returns for a client who overpaid about $47,000 in taxes because her bookkeeper and accountant did not track when she used her personal credit cards for business expenses. That's crazy! This chapter will teach you about some deductions you've never heard of

> *The first step is to look at deductions you are not currently using, or deductions that are slipping through the cracks.*

and some that your accountant may have said you can't write off (but you can!). Let's review some of the most common home-based business deductions. These will be brief summaries. If you want to learn more about each, check out our other book, *More Relaxing, Less Taxing for Network Marketers*.

Start-Up Costs

If you are in your first year of business, the costs you incurred before you began operations are deductible, up to $5,000. And if you spent more than $5,000, the costs are amortized over time.

Home Office Deduction

QuickBooks estimates that only about 33 percent of all self-employed individuals claim a home office deduction.

Many people avoid taking this obvious deduction because there are a lot of catches to it, and they think using it

Many people avoid taking this obvious deduction because there are a lot of catches to it, and they think using it can trigger an audit.

can trigger an audit. In reality, the IRS applies a simple two-part test:

- One, the dedicated space in your home must be used as your principal place of business, or it must have some other acceptable business purpose.

- Two, it must be used regularly and exclusively for the business. If you meet these criteria, then the applicable percentage of homeowner's insurance, mortgage interest or rent, repairs and maintenance, utility bills, and more, can all be deducted. Here's how this works: if your kitchen table doubles as your work desk, you cannot deduct it. However, if you have a dedicated room, or even a portion of a room, you can deduct some of your housing costs.

Example: A business owner uses 10 percent of his home for an office. – THIS NEEDS TO COME FROM MY 1ST BOOK.

	Expense	Home Office Percent	Deduction
Mortgage interest	$10,485	10%	$1,048.50
Real estate property tax	$1,800	10%	$180.00
Utilities	$3,975	10%	$397.50
Homeowners insurance	$1,500	10%	$150.00
Alarm system	$720	10%	$72.00
Home office repairs	$1,850	10%	$185.00
Depreciation of home	$2,500	10%	$250.00
Depreciation of furniture	$750	10%	$75.00
Tax Deductions			**$2,358.00**

Auto Expenses

If you travel to meet a client, perform a job outside your business, purchase business supplies, conduct research, or do any other kind of activity for your business, you can deduct these expenses. You have the option to write off the actual mileage based on your business use percentage, including gas, oil changes, car washes, maintenance and repairs, and depreciation, or you can take the standard mileage deductions. But with the new tax law changes passed in 2017, it is almost never a good idea to take the standard mileage method. Again, check out our other book, *More Relaxing Less Taxing for Network Marketers* to learn more about how to properly claim auto expenses for the greatest deduction.

So what qualifies as business driving? Many people believe that their drive to and from work is tax deductible, but this is not true. Your commute to your main office is not tax deductible. However, if you run a business from your home, then all your business stops from your home are deductible. So if you're going to the bank, you want to meet with a client, and you are going to pick up office supplies for your business, all are tax deductible if you have a regular job.

If you run a business from your home, then all your business stops from your home are deductible.

Healthcare Insurance Premiums

This is a deduction that is simply not available to employees. In most cases, because you are self-employed, you buy your own medical insurance. If this is the case, you can deduct 100% of what it costs to cover yourself and your family. This includes Medicare premiums. But there is a big exception for the self-employed. You can deduct what you pay for medical insurance for yourself and your family whether you itemize or not. This allows you to take a 100% deduction with no regard to the 7.5 percent threshold. You do not qualify if you are eligible for employer-sponsored health insurance through your job, if you are covered by a plan in addition to your business or covered through a spouse's job.

Retirement Plans

A retirement plan is one of the most profitable deductions for home-based business owners. Unlike employees, whose options are limited to whatever their employer offers, business owners can contribute pretax money to a simplified employee pension (SEP) or a solo 401(k), as well as an IRA. Your contributions to IRAs and 401(k) plans benefit you in two ways:

A retirement plan is one of the most profitable deductions for home-based business owners.

The first is that you can make annual salary deferrals of up to $18,500 and 25 percent of net income in 2018, plus an additional $6,000 if you're 50 or older, and it is tax deductible. Even better, you can contribute as much as 25 percent of your net earnings from self-employment (not including contributions for yourself), up to $55,000. The second benefit is that, because the money is tax-deferred, the government is rewarding you for creating your own retirement plan by not taxing you on the income until you withdraw the money further down the road.

Interest Payments

I constantly see that this is a huge missed tax deduction. From finance charges on a credit card to interest payments for vehicles, equipment, and loans—these things can be deducted. Business owners traditionally start operating with personal bank accounts, loans, and credit cards, and tend to forget to write off those interest charges.

Capital Expenditures

When you buy large items for your business (e.g., vehicles or computer systems) you have two choices regarding how to deduct the costs. The first is to depreciate the cost, deducting the expenses over a number of years, considered the "life" of the equipment or property. Depending on the situation, especially at the beginning of your business, where you may have losses, you have the option of writing off the equipment or property over multiple years, and this could possibly save you a great deal in years to come.

The second way is to expense the property or equipment using a Section 179 deduction. This allows you to deduct 100 percent of the qualifying cost up to your net income in the first year. In 2018, the new tax code increased the Section 179 deduction to $1 million worth of equipment eligible for immediate write-off (although the amount is reduced if you place more than $2.5 million of new assets into service during any single year). Be aware that if you claim depreciation for an automobile in a given tax year, you cannot switch back to claiming the standard mileage rate for the following tax year.

Education and Training

The cost of training classes, webinars, books, magazine subscriptions, research material, educational fees, travel, and other expenses related to business education and training are fully deductible. The greatest part about education is that it also grows your business by attending events or purchasing educational tools. For example, if you are in network marketing, the company you work with likely has its own events, and your attendance will improve your awareness of the company, your skills as a business owner, and it will expand your network of fellow network marketers. Or your investment in education and training could be personal development events such as those held by Les Brown, Tony Robbins, Eric Worre, or Grant Cardone. If you are attempting to grow your income, the events and tools you need to be successful are deductible!

The Pass-Through Entity Deduction

This is a new deduction that allows an additional 20 percent deduction for sole proprietorships, partnerships, and S-Corporations. This is huge for a business. *Example*: Your business makes $100,000 in net income. You only have to pay taxes on $80,000 because you receive $20,000 in a deduction due to the pass-through entity deduction.

Meals and Entertainment Have Changed Drastically

Eating out with a client can be a great way to grow your business. Did you know that many of your meals can be tax deductible? However, with the new tax law meals are still deductible—but entertainment is not. Please note you can no longer take clients out to sporting events such as golf or to a football or baseball game. The new law still allows for a 50 percent reduction of your meals. If you follow the rules, you will be able to deduct many of the meals you eat out. If you take a client out and spend $75 on a dinner and follow the rules outlined below, you can deduct 50 percent, or $37.50, of the meal. If you're in the 35 percent tax bracket, this will save you $13.13 in taxes at the end of the year. A meal qualifies as a deduction if it meets the following criteria:

1. You must have the appointment set up in advance, and whoever you're eating with must expect to talk about business.

2. You must talk about business before, during, or after the meal at any place that is easy to talk about business. The information must be recorded soon after the meal. The following information is crucial to your deduction: who did you take out to eat; where did you eat; when did the expense occur; what did you talk about; what was the expense, such as a meal or drinks; and finally, how much did the meal cost? Most of this information can be found on your receipt, other than who you took out and what you talked about.

Unfortunately, you are not able to deduct eating out with your spouse, even if they are a business partner and you discuss business. There are a few exceptions: if you take out a client and they bring along their spouse or significant other, you can bring your spouse or significant other, and up to 50% of your spouse's meal is deductible. However, if your client does not bring along a spouse or significant other, then your spouse's meal is not deductible—unless both of you are working on the project together.

Example: If both you and your spouse are mortgage brokers and will be helping out with the mortgage for your client's new home, then both of you are entitled to the 50 percent deduction.

CHAPTER 7

How to Hire Your Kids and Spouse and Lower Your Taxes

Hiring your kids

Kids are usually really expensive, but you can benefit from the expense of raising children by hiring your kids! If you own a business, there are things your children can do for you in your business.

A few examples:

- Posting to social media;
- Answering phones and emails to and from clients;
- Sending mailers, products, or samples;
- Filing paperwork;

- Cleaning the office;
- Helping with day-to-day transactions.

How can you do this? Well, if you were to hire an employee or a subcontractor to do any of the above, the expenses would be deductible, right? So why not hire your kids instead of someone else? Smart business owners realize children can be paid a reasonable wage if they do legitimate work for your business. They in turn can pay for what they want, such as video games or clothes. Not only do you benefit from the tax deductions, it teaches your kids how to manage their own money. Also, kids do not have to have pay taxes on the first $12,000 of income because of the new standard deduction. This is a true win-win for everyone.

> *Smart business owners realize children can be paid a reasonable wage if they do legitimate work for your business.*

Note that if you are treating your business like a sole proprietorship or partnership and your kids are under 18, there is no social security or unemployment taxes to deduct or match, and taxes do not have to be withheld if they are under the $12,000 income mark. If you have an S-Corp, you do have to withhold FICA taxes. There are ways around this as well, however. This is huge for you and your business. So hire your kids now instead of paying their bills! Courtney has six kids. If she paid them $12,000 per year (she's already spending it on them!), that would be $72,000 in deductions for her business, and they would not have to pay taxes.

Example: You pay your child $12,000 in wages for 2018 in your self-employed business. You are able to deduct wages of $12,000 on your Schedule C or Schedule E if it relates to rental property, assuming that those wages are reasonable. You would then pay no social security or unemployment taxes. Your child would report the $12,000 as income but then deduct the $12,000 standard deduction. If you are in a 39.6 percent tax bracket, this would produce a tax savings for you of $4,752 from federal taxes alone. If you paid your child more than $12,000 in wages, you would save 29.6 percent (39.6 percent minus the 10 percent bracket for children).

Your child could also put away $5,500 a year of the earnings into a Roth IRA that would allow the interest and appreciation of the IRA to be tax-free to the child if used for college. A lot of people wonder, "At what age can I hire my kids?" There is a tax court case that held that you could hire a child who is at least seven years old. If they are younger than seven, if you use social media and print advertising, hiring your child as a model may work. There is no precedent yet, but if you are willing to pay for stock photos and models, who says that you can't pay your kids instead? No one, yet!

The one thing that you must make sure of with your children is that you are paying them a reasonable salary and that you have a record of what they are doing for you in your business. What is reasonable? What are you willing to pay someone else to do the same job? If you would hire a bookkeeper for $15 an hour, you can hire your child to do the same for $13 an hour. This should be considered reasonable. Documentation is key when hiring relatives. There needs to be either a written or electronic time sheet that states:

- date worked;
- tasks performed; and
- hours worked.

The most important part is that you actually have to pay them! The money must go into an account, or you must be able to prove that they received payment. Make sure that you also have filled out the proper paperwork for employment, including a W-4, I-9, and that you have an employment application and contract. So go hire your kids and stop paying for their stuff—things like college, books, video games, and all the other things that kids want. Even "big kids"—those older than eighteen—qualify for this. You just have to pay the Social Security taxes, and so do they.

Hiring your spouse

Now let's talk about your spouse. When you hire your spouse, you must take out Social Security, so the key here is to pay them minimum wage and give them as many fringe benefits as possible. The main purpose of hiring your spouse is allowing the business to write off medical expenses that would not be deductible because of the threshold amount of 7.5 percent of your adjusted gross income (AGI). Self-employed people are not allowed to be covered under this plan, but that can be bypassed by

The main purpose of hiring your spouse is allowing the business to write off medical expenses that would not be deductible because of the threshold amount of 7.5 percent of your adjusted gross income (AGI).

hiring a spouse or forming a corporation and creating a self-insured medical plan that is in addition to medical insurance. This would cover copays, deductibles, coinsurance, dental, braces, medical miles, chiropractic, and more. The IRS allows that one employee is reasonable for a medical reimbursement account. You can reimburse your spouse for all medical expenses, and it would be considered a fringe benefit to him or her, so it would not be taxable for the spouse, and the business gets the deduction. The great part is that you get to maintain full control over the plan and can make it as broad or as narrow as you want.

> *The great part is that you get to maintain full control over the plan and can make it as broad or as narrow as you want.*

The steps required to set up a self-insured medical reimbursement plan are:

- Form a regular corporation and have the corporation approve the plan at a board of directors meeting;

- Have the medical reimbursement plan drafted;

- Make your spouse the primary insured on the plan and elect for family coverage;

- Pay the medical bills directly or reimburse any family member for any medical expense incurred;

- The plan needs to stay in existence for at least three years;

- Meet with your accountant annually to have a per year employee maximum payout to assure that the total salary and payout are reasonable for the hours and work performed.

Remember, you can only utilize these deductions after the plan has been implemented. Also, you must make sure that you do not discriminate in favor of the owners, so if you have other employees, you must cover all full-time employees, meaning the plan must cover 70 percent or more of all employees. There are exceptions to this rule, including part-time workers, employees under twenty-five years of age, employees with less than three years of service, and nonresident aliens.

We realize this was a lot of technical information to take in, and we barely scratched the surface, especially with fringe benefits for companies with employees, like employer-provided vacations, gym equipment, and weekly team lunches. For more information about tax deductions, check out our other book, *More Relaxing Less Taxing for Network Marketer*!

CHAPTER 8

Real Life Client Savings
(Whose story compares to yours?)

So often we plan our lives to fit a certain narrative. We love the idea of being self-employed and not answering to anyone else in business. We romanticize what it will be like to have time flexibility and financial stability. We feel this drive to execute our vision and we jump in with both feet. We carefully plan for marketing expenses and software costs. We have this amazing spreadsheet that we built that is the answer to where all our money is being used in the creation of our entrepreneurial dream. Then tax time comes, and we are completely lost as to why we have to pay so much of our hard-earned money to Uncle Sam.

Well, the reality is whether you are employed by someone else or you are self-employed and own a home-based business, you are likely paying too much on your taxes. Courtney has helped thousands of people save money on

> *Well, the reality is whether you are employed by someone else or you are self-employed and own a home-based business, you are likely paying too much on your taxes.*

their taxes. The average person who comes to her firm saves between $4,000 and $8,000 dollars off their taxes compared the previous year as long as nothing drastic has changed. For many of her clients the story is much, much better than that.

She's going to share some real-life examples of clients and their very real savings. As you read through these, choose one that most closely resembles your own situation. For simplicity, these stories are written in order of smallest to largest refunds, and for privacy, their last names have been changed.

Linda – Linda had never owned a business before. She was a W2 employee most of her adult life and was recently introduced to relationship marketing but hadn't made much money from it. It was too early in Linda's entrepreneurial journey to incur the cost of setting up a new entity for her, so we simply did her taxes and gave her a road map to help her start saving even more on her taxes going forward. We were still able to save Linda $2900 on her taxes.

Jessica - Jessica and her husband have been W2 employees their entire life. They found relationship marketing two years before, and they were not extremely successful. We were able to save them $4100 more in taxes than they ever saved before because they were able to redirect their living expenses and turn those into business expenses.

Lisa – Lisa had been extremely successful in the network marketing industry but felt that every year she was paying way too much in taxes. She did not feel that her accounting was helping her in anyway even though they were handling her bookkeeping and taxes. We were able to save Lisa almost 40K a year for three years, due to overpaying herself in a paycheck from her company and missing deductions that her accountant did not write off.

John – John's prior accountant was not tracking all of his business expenses and was also having him overpay in payroll taxes and was missing out on expenses as his accountant did not understand the network marketing industry. We amended these returns and were able to save him $57K in taxes.

Wendy – Wendy had an e-commerce business and a network marketing business. Her prior accountant not only had her paying herself and her husband too much in a paycheck, which cost them thousands in payroll taxes that was not necessary. We also were able to restructure one of her businesses and track deductions correctly saving her $110K per year for three years.

Courtney could go on and on with different examples. After helping thousands of people pay an accurate amount of taxes, one thing grew clear: taxes are the one area of business that people understand the least, overpay the most, and are extremely grateful for any help someone is able to give them. Needless to say, she loves what she does.

CHAPTER 9

How to Structure Your Business for the Greatest Tax Savings

When first starting a business, people tend to operate as cheaply as possible. Because of this, they may start operating the business in their personal name and not a business name. Some may go as far as getting an LLC but still claim their income through their personal tax return.

However, especially for tax purposes, there is a benefit to providing more structure to your business, and it's relatively easy and painless. In this chapter, we'll explore the different types of business entities you can choose from, as well as the advantages and disadvantages for each. We're going to share with you what we feel the best entity is for the majority of businesses, especially small to medium sized ones.

Sole Proprietorship

A sole proprietorship is by far the most popular entity for home-based business owners, but that does not necessarily make it the best option for you. Most people get started with a sole proprietorship because it is cheap and easy. It is the default option for operating a business because you don't actually create a separate business entity. A sole proprietorship allows you to operate a business as yourself, and you claim your business income and expenses on your personal tax return on Schedule C.

The Benefits

A sole proprietorship is easy and simple to form. Your sole proprietorship is already established once you start incurring expenses, and you are officially in business when you make your first sale. There may be business license requirements in your city or county, but there are no required filings for a city, county, or state return. You would use your Social Security number, and you are not even required to have a tax ID number unless you are going to have sales tax or payroll filings.

The Disadvantages

There are three major issues when it comes to sole proprietorship:

1. exposure to liability;
2. self-employment tax; and
3. audit risk.

Neither of us is an attorney, nor do we claim to be one, but almost everyone knows that if you are a sole proprietor, your personal assets are completely exposed when operating your business, meaning if something were to go wrong and you were sued, all of your personal assets (your home, your car, your belongings, etc.) could be used to settle a lawsuit.

The second downside is self-employment taxes for sole proprietors are 15.3 percent on their net income under $100,000 and 2.9 percent on anything above that. This is a huge amount of money that most sole proprietors don't even realize they owe. It is extremely important for sole proprietors to maximize their expenses so they can keep their income down as much as possible. It is also extremely important to monitor your income if you are a sole proprietor to make sure that you convert to an S-Corporation, or create an LLC and treat it as an S-Corp for tax purposes, saving you tens of thousands of dollars. I suggest that you should have an LLC once you are making $1,000 a month in gross income and that you convert that LLC to an S Corporation once you are making $1000-1500 per month in net income.

$100,000 Revenue
– $25,000 Expenses
= $75,000 Net Income. At 15.3 percent self-employment tax = $11,475

This is on top of state and federal taxes! Along with the liability, you can see that being a sole proprietor can really cost you more than you could ever pay to set up your business as an LLC or S-Corp if you are generating income.

The third problem is that sole proprietors are the most likely to be audited by the IRS. If you are going to be more aggressive with your tax write-offs, we would not recommend operating as a sole proprietorship.

When Does It Work?

The first instance in which a sole proprietorship works is when you are just getting started with a business idea and you are not sure where it is headed. If you are not operat-

> *The first instance in which a sole proprietorship works is when you are just getting started with a business idea and you are not sure where it is headed.*

ing fully, it can be too much to set up a formal company at the start. However, once liability becomes a concern and you are committed to what you are doing, you need to consult an accountant and attorney to consider which entity is best for you and your situation.

The second instance when it makes sense is when you are hiring your children who are under eighteen. This would be extremely helpful in saving additional taxes. This type of company is called a *family support company*, and it charges your formal business entities to provide support and management services. Then, you don't have to deduct

FICA taxes of 7.65 percent from your kids, and you don't have to pay the matching 7.65 percent FICA taxes.

The second instance when it makes sense is when you are hiring your children who are under eighteen.

Example: You have three kids under eighteen and pay them $12,000 per year in income. This would save your children $918 each in FICA taxes and save the company $2,754 in matching FICA taxes. Understand that there may be other licenses that are needed. You may need a business license for your state, city, or county. If you have payroll, you will also have to obtain a federal and state ID number as well as an unemployment tax ID number. You will want to consult an accountant or attorney to make sure this is all set up properly. Also, I suggest you not go with an incorporation service. There are many questions that need to be answered and instructions that you should receive with the formation of your first company.

Partnerships

The Benefits

The same benefits apply to partnerships as do sole proprietorships. They are easy and simple to form. You will need a federal ID number as there is a separate partnership return that will need to be filed.

The Disadvantages

Again, the main disadvantages of a partnership are risk and liability: the worst part of having a partnership is the liability that you are personally responsible for—not only for your actions but the actions of your partner. It is bad enough to be liable for what you do and can control, but to be liable for someone else is an entirely different ball game.

Again, the main disadvantages of a partnership are risk and liability: the worst part of having a partnership is the liability that you are personally responsible for—not only for your actions but the actions of your partner.

Example: If your partner goes to the bank and borrows $25,000 in the name of the business, you are liable to pay that back if the partner does not. Also, taxes for the business are 100 percent owed by both parties until one party—or both—pay their share.

You also have the same exposure to self-employment taxes as the sole proprietor. Make sure if you choose this route that you have a proper operating agreement in place. We've seen one too many clients who went into business with friends and family and did not have an operating agreement and ended up in tax debt, personal debt, and/or did not receive their share of what was owed to them.

S-Corporation
The Benefits

This is by far our favorite entity: the S-Corporation. One of the greatest things about this entity is that the IRS allows you to be an LLC but to be treated as an S-Corporation for tax purposes. Most of Courtney's clients are an LLC treated as an S-Corp. However, she has others that are true S-Corporations. There are many benefits. The number-one benefit is to allow you to save on self-employment taxes. Those with an S-Corporation are required to take a reasonable salary, and the remainder is just included in their bottom line. What is a reason-

Those with an S-Corporation are required to take a reasonable salary, and the remainder is just included in their bottom line.

able salary? What would you be willing to pay someone to replace you? Usually, 30% of your net income is a good number to pay payroll on, but when you have a low income, you should claim a higher rate.

Example: If your net income is $36,000 and you work full-time in your business, you may want to claim $15,000. If you are making $75,000 in net income, we would suggest $25,000. Make sure you speak with your tax strategist to ensure you are claiming what you should. There is no corporate tax or self-employment tax on the net income of an S-Corporation. Through a K-1, which is part of the 1120S, it flows through to the personal tax return, and taxes are paid on your Form 1040.

$100,000 Revenue
– $25,000 Salary at 15.3 percent self-employment tax
– 25,000 Expenses
= $50,000 Net Income

With this example, $50,000 would flow through your personal tax return without paying self-employment taxes of 15.3 percent. The tax savings are $7,650. This is *huge* for a small business. And that money could be used to grow the company, for retirement, or could help put your kids through college. The second reason is asset protection. Just like a C-Corporation, if the owners and operators act within their responsibilities and the duties of the company, there is no personal liability from the business operations.

The Disadvantages

There aren't a lot of downsides for an S-Corporation, but it does require more paperwork. You must pay yourself a paycheck. You also must pay payroll taxes and file payroll tax returns quarterly. Also, payroll taxes must be paid. The cost to set up an S-Corporation is higher than a Sole Proprietorship or LLC, but the benefits definitely outweigh the price. The last is that this is not a great entity to hold property in and later sell at an appreciated value. Also, if you have partners, it is tough to distribute partnership profits

The cost to set up an S-Corporation is higher than a Sole Proprietorship or LLC, but the benefits definitely outweigh the price.

to help with tax planning. There are better ways to set this up. Speak with a tax strategist on your individual situation.

When Does It Work?

When you need asset protection, you have a strong reason to set up an S-Corporation. As S-Corp is also preferable when you start making a net income in your business and the self-employment tax savings are higher than the cost of establishing an S-Corporation. It's usually feasible at about $25,000 in net income.

When you need asset protection, you have a strong reason to set up an S-Corporation.

Limited Liability Company, or LLC

The Benefits

An LLC is used mainly to store assets. They limit your personal liability to the business. There is also an option to set up an LLC and treat it as an S-Corporation for tax purposes. This is the greatest thing for Courtney's clients, as LLCs are not as expensive to get started as an S-Corp, and it allows for massive self-employment tax savings. Another benefit of an LLC is it's easier to handle profit and losses for partners, as this type of entity is treated as a partnership if there are partners. Partners are not liable for each other's actions if you use an LLC.

When Does It Make Sense?

Filing as an LLC makes sense if you have any property, including rental, investment, or commercial. Secondly, it makes sense when you go into partnership with someone to limit the liability.

Filing as an LLC makes sense if you have any property, including rental, investment, or commercial. Secondly, it makes sense when you go into partnership with someone to limit the liability.

Please take time to get a tax consultation before setting up your business, as setup is crucial. LLCs are great as they are easy to set up—but not so easy to unwind.

Summary: In Courtney's opinion, after eighteen years of experience, she finds that the greatest flexibility with the best savings is to file as an LLC and to treat it as an S-Corporation for tax purposes by requesting the S-Corp Election. This allows her clients to get the

> *The greatest flexibility with the best savings is to file as an LLC and to treat it as an S-Corporation for tax purposes by requesting the S-Corp Election.*

self-employment tax savings and does not cost them as much as an S-Corporation. Their liability is also limited, making this a great entity type.

CHAPTER 10

Audit-Proofing Your Business

Courtney's Audit-Proofing Crash Course

Does the word *audit* make you break out in a nervous sweat? That's OK. Courtney here, and I'm going to guide you through every step of how to get through this and make sure you are audit-proofing your books. You must understand first that being selected to be audited does not mean that the IRS or Department of Revenue believes you have done something wrong. If you are a business owner, you have a 73 percent likelihood that you will be audited at least one time in a 20-year period, according to tax attorney and CPA Sandy Botkin.

Thankfully, I have only had a couple of clients audited during my eighteen years in accounting. But I have helped handle numerous others, including one that lasted for seven days. I learned a lot in the room with that auditor

You must understand first that being selected to be audited does not mean that the IRS or Department of Revenue believes you have done something wrong.

and what they were actually looking for, and I now share that insight with my clients.

The first thing the auditor asked my client was: "What would it cost you to replace yourself?" My client immediately said, "Well, at least $60,000 a year." Next, the auditor asked her to determine if she was paying herself a reasonable salary. I stress this: *never answer this question*, especially if you have not been paying yourself at

"What would it cost you to replace yourself?"

all. Once she said $60,000, my client was going to get hit with 25 percent for not paying herself a paycheck, and then she would have to pay self-employment of 15.3 percent, and federal and state, which is another 29 percent (in her situation). That is an extra $41,000 in taxes. I had advised my client not to answer any questions before I arrived, and that one question was going to cost her $41,000, times two, as her 2013 and 2014 returns were being audited.

I ended up working with the auditor and explaining that my client does not work in the business on a day-to-day basis, that what she does consists of ten to fifteen hours per week, and that someone could be paid ten dollars an hour to do the same work. We derived a yearly income of $18,000, which was only $12,400 in taxes. *Huge difference.* So, make sure you have a competent accountant who is working with you through your audit and that the accountant is going to be there to answer all questions.

I am not telling you to lie—by no means am I saying that—but there are things in the tax code that you may not understand, and you would be much better off allowing an accountant to handle those issues than yourself. Do not give more information than you have been asked, either. The most important thing to understand about

Do not give more information than you have been asked.

an audit is that you do not want to ignore the audit! This will make you look as if you're trying to hide something. All interviews for audits are going to be in person. You will receive paperwork in the mail that you are required to respond to and provide documentation for. If you do not have everything that they are requesting, don't panic! There are certain parts of the tax code that we help you with if you don't have receipts under $75 but be sure to provide everything you have that is requested of you. This could include mileage logs, receipts, general ledgers, P&L statements, and balance sheets.

Also, you want to make sure the IRS has your correct address in the event that you move. This could cause a major issue if you are audited and do not receive the audit request documents. This happened to me, as I had moved. I had no clue that my tax return was being audited, and the paperwork was not forwarded to me. It took me three and a half years to resolve this matter; I had to request to reopen the audit, then appeal the audit, and finally the IRS released my $23,000 refund (they had taken my refund every year for three years). To change your address, you will need to fill out an 8822 form, which is a change of address form. Not filling out this form will cost you a lot of time and more effort on your part, since the paperwork will not get to you, and you will have to track it down from the IRS or state agencies. It could also cause your refund to be held up. It could take up to nine months for the IRS to release a new check for your refund.

It is imperative that you send your tax return electronically. This will not only get you your refund faster, it's proof that your tax return has been filed. You want to make sure you have a competent tax preparer doing your taxes. It definitely helps if you are audited to have someone to rely on instead of yourself. A tax software will not go to an audit for you! It is important as well that your tax preparer is available year-round for you to ask questions

It is imperative that you send your tax return electronically.

and help with tax matters as the issues usually come up long after-tax season is over. I would advise that you don't do your own tax returns; the IRS realizes that you are more likely to create errors than a tax professional, and that could increase your chances of being audited. Also, one tax strategy session with a competent accountant will enlighten you, likely, on thousands of dollars that you are not taking in tax deductions.

I have had clients miss $50,000 in expenses in one year by trying to put together their own P&Ls for a tax preparer. *What you don't know will cost you.* If you are given expert advice on a particular deduction or item, please make sure that you keep a record of that item, because if that advice is found to be incorrect, having the record could save you penalties and interest.

You should never brag to anyone that you have not paid taxes or filed your returns. There may be a legitimate

You should never brag to anyone that you have not paid taxes or filed your returns.

reason behind both of these, but you must know that the failure to file a tax return when you owe money is considered tax evasion and is illegal. If someone gets angry with you and decides to contact the IRS, there is—believe this or not—a 30 percent finder's fee for people who turn you in. (You can find this information in IRS Publication 733.) Among those who turn people in, it is often angry ex-boyfriends or ex-girlfriends, ex-spouses, and ex-employees. Watch what you say, because it can be used against you.

The IRS has implemented numerous sophisticated software programs to find people who don't report all of their income. Don't try to hide your income from them.

> # *The IRS has implemented numerous sophisticated software programs to find people who don't report all of their income.*

The IRS has implemented numerous sophisticated software programs to find people who don't report all of their income.

This is illegal. Not paying all that you owe, however, is tax avoidance. Although frowned upon, it is not illegal. There are a couple of myths I would like to address about audits:

1. That you are more likely to be audited if you take certain deductions, such as business use of your home or car expenses. This is not true, and if you are

entitled to the deductions, you should take them! There is no reason for you to give the government more money than it is entitled to receive. What can potentially trigger an audit is if your income drastically increases or decreases.

2. That audits are done immediately. It usually takes two years before you receive anything from the IRS in reference to an audit or similar issues that are taking place.

3. That professionally filed returns are audit-proof. This is just not true but taking this step definitely does help eliminate errors that could cause you to be audited. Again, it is best to e-file your return, and it is always a great idea to have an accountant prepare your return.

4. That you should be extremely afraid of an audit. This is just not true. (Though, understand, I am not saying audits are fun.) Understand that an audit is just to determine that the information on your return can be proven. The biggest reason people lose on audits is because they don't have the receipts or backup to prove their expenses. Auditors like backup. I've also found that you have a much better chance if you have an accounting software such as QuickBooks so that you can provide the auditor with a general ledger, P&L, and balance sheet that ties back to your tax return.

The two most valuable pieces of advice I can give you when it comes to your taxes are:

1. Choose someone to do your taxes who will be on your side in the event of an audit, and

2. Track everything. Nothing will serve you better in an audit than good record keeping.

Let's discuss the first point. Choosing the right person to do your taxes is one of the most important financial decisions of your life. Consider how much you will pay in taxes over your lifetime. It is often one of the single

Choosing the right person to do your taxes is one of the most important financial decisions of your life.

largest expenses we'll ever pay. Doesn't it make sense to have the right person in your corner? You need to have someone who really understands small businesses and the parts of the tax code that directly affects them. It is not enough to have someone who knows how to file taxes, you need someone who knows how to guide you through the process and be there with you through an audit if that were to happen. This brings us to point number two, good record keeping. Unless you are the most organized person on the planet, you will need the support of a record keeping app like TaxBot. TaxBot will allow you to take pictures of receipts the moment the expense is incurred. It gets filed and applied to the accurate category with a stored picture for proof to back it up. TaxBot also tracks your mileage automatically so you can maximize the benefits granted to you under mileage deductions.

If You Are Audited

One of the most important things to understand is that you need to assume you are going to be audited when you prepare your tax return. You need to keep six years' worth

One of the most important things to understand is that you need to assume you are going to be audited when you prepare your tax return.

of data and be able to easily find and explain that information to an auditor. If you simply keep the documents with your tax return records from year to year, it makes things much easier if you are selected to be audited. You want to make sure that you do not, in any way, try to avoid an auditor. You will make the auditor believe you are hiding something, and then they may become overly zealous trying to find something that you could be leaving out.

You Have Not Done Anything Wrong if You Are Audited

It simply means that the government is requesting more information. You want to make sure that you only bring the information that is requested by the auditor, because you do not want to trigger a red flag on something else that the auditor is not looking for. You also must understand that you have to prove your deductions are valid. The IRS does not have to prove anything, and this is where it becomes crucial to keep a good accounting of all your deductions. You should be prepared to answer questions, and it's an excellent idea to have a competent accountant do this for you. Make sure that you are organized, as your auditor is going to think that your return doesn't have sufficient backup if you are disorganized, and that will, once again, start a fishing expedition. This can result in more in-depth audits or going back prior years for auditing. The more organized you are, the faster your audit is going to be.

If you disagree with the auditor, do not argue with him or her. If you think you are right, however, ask the auditor or agent for the legal reference. Do not accept vague statements as interpretations of the law.

If you disagree with the auditor, do not argue with him or her.

Tell them, "My accountant told me that this deduction is proper. Can you give me something to show that he's wrong?" However, do not, in any manner, get in an argument with an auditor. If you have an issue that you cannot resolve, ask for their supervisor's contact information.

Lastly, you should never tamper with evidence or lie to an agent. This is a federal offense. Understand as well that your accountant has no privilege protecting your communication on criminal matters. Any communication with

Lastly, you should never tamper with evidence or lie to an agent.

your accountant can be obtained by the IRS in a criminal matter. And you *never* want to be alone with a special agent. These people are not "special" in any way. Their one and only job is to investigate criminal activities. You will want to seek a criminal tax attorney, immediately, to help with this matter. If you do decide to talk, understand that it is easier for the government to prove that you are lying to a federal official than it is to get you on the crime itself!

A few more things you want to be aware of if you are audited: you should dress normally and be on time for the audit. Auditors don't like people who act and look as if they have no money, and, in the same way, they don't like people who act and look like they have more money than they do. Just be normal, be yourself. Auditors are graded on their efficiency. If you are late for your appointment and cause the auditor to be inefficient in what he or she is doing, you are definitely starting off on the wrong foot. If you are late, it gives the auditor more time to examine your return and see if they can find any issues. You do not, in any way, want to give in too quickly. Auditors will believe you are trying to hide something if you agree to adjustments too quickly. The IRS may actually look *further* into deductions if you seem too eager to end an audit. You have many rights as a taxpayer, and you should know those rights. Make sure you are as aggressive with your deductions as possible, but also make sure you have your backup information if you are audited.

Make sure you have your backup information if you are audited.

Also, statistics show you are two- to twenty-times more likely to be audited if you have a Schedule C business as opposed to an LLC treated as an S-Corporation. This is still one more reason to have an S-Corporation.

CHAPTER 11

Business with Heart: The Power of Social Business

Now that we've gone through the nitty gritty details of taxes, audits, and the technical aspects of saving through a home-based business, we'd like to return to the bigger picture.

We both love building sustainable businesses that give us financial flexibility. But there's actually more to it than that. We mentioned early on that one of the benefits of owning a home-based business is the ability to give back and create a sense of purpose. For most people, they go to work, come home with only a few hours of the day to spend with their family, then rinse and repeat. Any time off is used for personal vacations, and other small ways to enjoy all the work you've done. This is the working life

One of the benefits of owning a home-based business is the ability to give back and create a sense of purpose.

we've been trained to expect. But what about a sense of purpose? A feeling of being connected to something bigger than ourselves, or giving back in a way that's meaningful?

When you have your own business, you get to be the master behind its design, and something we've discovered that has truly made all the difference in our working lives is what's called a social business. A social business has an added objective of serving a social or environmental cause. It's not about being a nonprofit—you can make as much profit as you want! It's about the spirit behind additional endeavors your business can enable. What causes are you passionate about? What good do you want to do in the world?

One of the secrets to happiness is to discover a purpose outside yourself, to find ways to use all of your knowl-

One of the secrets to happiness is to discover a purpose outside yourself.

edge, tenacity, and a willingness to step outside the box to do good for your family and for others.

We'd each like to take a moment to share how building a socially responsible mission behind our businesses has been important to us. And if you start a home-based business, you might just find an additional life of purpose and impact, too.

Courtney

Exactly two year ago, I was able to make a shift in my thinking and my business, and I realized that I am what Tony Robbins calls an artist. That means that I just really love what I do and have a passion to help people and make my craft better. That craft so happens to be accounting and tax strategy for small- to medium-sized businesses.

The shift happened because I attended an event that Tony Robbins was at, and I realized the gift I had was unlike any other accountant I had ever met. I realized my gift came to me through the school of hard knocks. Because I had failed in business and succeeded in different types of business, my skill set was completely different than that of a typical accountant. I am first and foremost an entrepreneur, and I have learned through business more about accounting than I think I ever would have sitting in a cubicle at an accounting firm.

Through my search to not only find great tax deductions but also improve my health and wealth, I was introduced to a company that allowed me to get healthy, lose weight, make some extra money, and have more tax deductions. I was also introduced to a concept called social business, which completely transformed my way of thinking. It made me want to strive to not only be better for myself but to also strive for a much bigger purpose than simply my own.

I was also introduced to a concept called social business, which completely transformed my way of thinking. It made me want to strive to not only be better for myself but to also strive for a much bigger purpose than simply my own.

I did not fully understand the concept at first, and I really thought it was a sales tactic from this company to sell more products. When I truly started to get involved in the process and realized what a difference I was making, it caused me to make another shift.

My purpose went from providing for my family and myself and helping clients to also working to eradicate childhood malnutrition. I was also able to meet one of the most amazing men I have ever met. His name is Sam Caster, and he is the founder of MannaRelief. I have partnered with them because I love their purpose. Also, the fact that I am giving based upon my gross income from my business allows me to write off 100 percent of the proceeds given to MannaRelief as a cost of goods sold.

I would suggest that you find something you are passionate about and give to that cause. When your passion and profits meet, it will create something inside you like nothing else can. God has truly blessed our family since we started giving to MannaRelief on April 15, 2018.

When your passion and profits meet, it will create something inside you like nothing else can.

MannaRelief is the only nonprofit in the world that provides whole food nourishment to children in need. We are now providing a daily nourishment for every $1 that we bring into our accounting practice. There is nothing else like the feeling of knowing that because of our business and that decision, not only are we helping our clients and providing for ourselves, we are providing nourishment to more than 9,000 children a day.

At the time of this book's publishing, MannaRelief has provided more than 130 million servings of food to children in need in ninety different countries and given needed nutrition to more than ten thousand medically fragile children, which helps their bodies fight sickness and disease, and heal, in dramatic ways.

We are also very proud of our partnership with Operation Underground Railroad. They help children escape from sex trafficking as well as provide aftercare for these vulnerable children. In 2019 alone, they were able to free 3,000 children. You can find out more about their initiative at ourrescue.org.

The Last Well is another organization that we provide for. They are doing a border-to-border initiative in Liberia to provide safe drinking water to every village in that country while sharing the gospel. They have been working on this mission for the last 11 years and will have provided water for every person in Liberia as of Dec 31, 2020, a total of 5.2 million people. Once Liberia is finished, they will begin another border-to-border initiative. You can gain more understanding of what they are doing at thelastwell.org.

Robert

About 10 years ago I was blessed with the best job one could possibly have on the corporate side of the relationship marketing profession. I was hired as the VP of sales for a startup MLM. My role was vast. I was responsible for making sure the compensation plan would elicit the proper behaviors, all marketing and communications, video production, recognition, events and presentations (both writing them and delivering them), building the field of independent representatives from scratch, and training the same. I was even in charge of compliance. It really just depended on the situation that was happening at the time as to which hat, I had to put on. When I was hired, the company had about 30 customers and not one single distributor to grow the business. That is where I come in. My job was to grow the field of independent reps so they could grow the customer book of the company. It was an exciting time. All my roles during this chapter of my life were challenging and fulfilling at the same time. But nothing I was tasked to do was more core to who I was as a person than the social good aspect of the business that I got to develop. I came up with the concept that we called "7 Continents in 7 Years". The idea was to visit each of the 7 continents over the next 7 years and (1) do a service project to bless the lives of those who lived in the community we were about to visit, and then part two when the service was done was (2) party like rock stars in a very resort-esque area of the same country. Our first location we chose to serve was in Brazil. I chose it because I am fluent in Portuguese, no other reason. I figured if I was going to host 30 people in a foreign country, I should at least be able to speak the language.

Let me explain a little further. So much of what we do in MLM is centered on ranking up in the business. What one needs to do in order to advance to the next rank or "Pin Level"? We are consumed with the daily rituals of prospecting, inviting, showing the plan, and following up. Don't get me wrong, I love that side of the business and have earned a great deal of income honing people's skills in those areas. But the social good part is what I live for.

What one needs to do in order to advance to the next rank or "Pin Level"? We are consumed with the daily rituals of prospecting, inviting, showing the plan, and following up.

Follow along with me for a minute, and I'll set the stage for you. Imagine you are brand-new to your new side hustle, and at your very first presentation the guy at the front of the room (me) tells you how much work it's going to take to earn an international trip to some far-off exotic place. I mean you are going to have to sacrifice and really put your shoulder to the wheel to earn one of these truly once-in-a-lifetime trip—and when you do, after all that effort, blood, sweat, and tears you put in to earn it, that after all that, when you get there, to this exotic place far away.... you are going to do a service project! Yep, you get to work hard to then go work hard again. Who would have ever thought that people would bust their tails to then go bust their tails? The reality is these were the best of times. These are the trips we still talk about today.

After 10 years of doing these social good service trips all over the world, no one ever seems to talk about, "I got to lay by a pool in Bali for eight days; it was the best trip ever." *No way!* When you can say, "I got to play soccer with local children on a dirt field in a mountain village on the side of a volcano in a remote area of Guatemala." Now you're livin'. Think about being able to serve a family in an underdeveloped country in some remote place in the world and give your heart to them, expecting nothing in return—that is when you find yourself. One of my favorite quotes is, "It is often in our extremities that we come to know God." I just think when you give a part of yourself and expect nothing in return you are acting as Christlike as we are programmed to be. Over the years I have done service trips like I described here, twice in Guatemala where we did a clean cookstove project and a clean water project; two different trips that just meant

Think about being able to serve a family in an underdeveloped country in some remote place in the world and give your heart to them, expecting nothing in return— that is when you find yourself.

the world to me. I was able to serve the same family each time. On the first trip we built them a clean cookstove and when we returned, we were able to gift them a clean water cistern or "tinoco" as they called it.

I just think when you give a part of yourself and expect nothing in return you are acting as Christlike as we are programmed to be.

I have been to the Philippines twice. Both trips we worked on rehabbing orphanages in the town of Ormoc on Leyte Island. A piece of my heart will always be in the Philippines with the children there that we were able to serve. I would have come home with two or three of them if they would have

> *"You fall in love with those you serve."*
> —Robert A. McFadden

let me. Ormoc, Philippines; Ghana, Africa; Tehran, Albania; Gold Coast, Australia; Manaus, Brazil; Navajo Nation, USA; and the list goes on. I have been blessed to continue these style trips all over the world, want to come on the next one? Reach out to me at rob@robertamcfadden.com and we'll get you registered. Each place we served the families and communities, expected nothing in return. I am a better person for these service trips. I have been blessed to have been able to take my wife and children on several of these experiences, and we are stronger and more grounded because of it. All these experiences were made possible by and because of the MLM profession. I'll end with this regarding serving others. You fall in love with those you serve. PERIOD. To this

You fall in love with those you serve. PERIOD. To this day I cannot meet a single person from one of the areas I have done a service project and not have an immediate connection with them.

day I cannot meet a single person from one of the areas I have done a service project and not have an immediate connection with them. I want to be their friend, and they can do no wrong in my eyes from the moment a rapport is built.

If your business does not drive you to do good for others, then you are in the wrong business!

CORPORATE RETURN DEDUCTION INFORMATION

NAME

WHEN DID YOUR BUSINESS START?

ANNUAL INCOME

PRODUCT/SERVICE TYPE?

BUSINESS ADDRESS (IF NOT THE SAME AS YOUR HOME)

Have you depreciated any assets in the last year? ☐ **YES** ☐ **NO**
• If 'YES' attach your deprecation schedules.

CITY   STATE   ZIP

COMPENSATION OF OFFICERS AND SHAREHOLDER INFORMATION

NAME

NAME

ADDRESS

ADDRESS

CITY   STATE   ZIP

CITY   STATE   ZIP

PHONE NUMBER

PHONE NUMBER

EMAIL ADDRESS

EMAIL ADDRESS

TAX ID NUMBER   NUMBER OF SHARES

TAX ID NUMBER   NUMBER OF SHARES

NAME

NAME

ADDRESS

ADDRESS

CITY   STATE   ZIP

CITY   STATE   ZIP

PHONE NUMBER

PHONE NUMBER

EMAIL ADDRESS

EMAIL ADDRESS

TAX ID NUMBER   NUMBER OF SHARES

TAX ID NUMBER   NUMBER OF SHARES

DEDUCTIONS CONTINUED ON NEXT PAGE...

DEDUCTION SPREADSHEETS

BUSINESS SOLUTIONS

HOME BASED/NETWORK MARKETING INFORMATION

NAME

PRODUCT/SERVICE TYPE?

BUSINESS ADDRESS (IF NOT THE SAME AS YOUR HOME)

ANNUAL INCOME   WHEN DID YOUR BUSINESS START?

CITY   STATE   ZIP

Have you depreciated any assets in the last year? ☐ YES ☐ NO
- If 'YES" attach your deprecation schedules.

EXPENSES	
Childcare*	
Cell Phone Bill/Telephone	
Internet Services	
Electronics for Business/Software	
Printing/Copying	
Office Supplies	
Coaching/Consulting	
Advertising/Marketing	
Passport	
Postage	
Dues	
Clothing/Dry Cleaning	
Travel	
Meals 50%	
Meals 100%	
Gifts/Prizes/Contests	
Payroll Taxes for Employees	
Tax Preparation/Book Keeping	
Continuing Education/Training	
Cost of Goods Sold/Supplies	
Legal Fees	
Subcontractors	
Liability/Worker's Compensation	
Medical Insurance*	
Wages	
Interest Expense	
Bank Charges	
Event Expenses	
TOTAL:	

*REQUIRES PLAN

HOME INFORMATION	
Sq. Ft. of Home	
Sq. Ft. of Office	
Cost of Home	
BUSINESS USE OF YOUR HOME	
Real Estate Taxes	
Mortgage Interest or Rent	
HOA Fees	
Utilities	
Repairs and Maintenance	
Depreciation Expense	
Homeowners Insurance	
TOTAL:	

AUTOMOBILE INFORMATION	
Business Miles (current tax year)	
Vehicle Make	
Vehicle Model	
Vehicle Year	
Date of Purchase	
Cost of Vehicle	
AUTO EXPENSES	
What is your % of Business Usage?	
Gas	
Oil Changes	
Auto Insurance	
Repairs and Maintenance	
Interest Expenses	
Vehicle Taxes	
TOTAL:	

FEDERAL TAXES ALREADY PAID	DATE:	AMOUNT:
1st Quarter		
2nd Quarter		
3rd Quarter		
4th Quarter		

STATE TAXES ALREADY PAID	DATE:	AMOUNT:
1st Quarter		
2nd Quarter		
3rd Quarter		
4th Quarter		

BUSINESS SOLUTIONS

FOR OFFICE USE ONLY

DATE RECEIVED: _____
INITIALS: _____

RENTAL PROPERTY DEDUCTIONS

COMPANY NAME

TAX PAYER NAME

PROPERTY ADDRESS

CITY

COUNTY   **STATE**   **ZIP**

DATE OF PROPERTY PURCHASE   **TAXABLE YEAR**

INCOME FROM PROPERTY

TYPE OF PROPERTY:
- ☐ SINGLE FAMILY RESIDENCE
- ☐ MULTI-FAMILY RESIDENCE
- ☐ VACATION/SHORT-TERM RENTAL
- ☐ COMMERCIAL
- ☐ LAND
- ☐ ROYALTIES
- ☐ SELF-RENTAL
- ☐ OTHER (DESCRIBE) _____

EXPENSES	
Advertising	
Auto and Travel	
Cleaning and Maintenance	
Commissions	
Insurance	
Legal and Other Professional Fees	
Management Fees	
Mortgage Interest Paid to Banks, etc.	
Other Interest	
Repairs	
Supplies	
Taxes	
Utilities	
Depreciation Expense or Depletion	
Other	
TOTAL:	

PROPERTY INFORMATION	
Sq. Ft. of Home	
Cost of Home	
RENTAL DAYS (MUST EQUAL 365)	
Fair Rental Days	
Personal Use Days	
PROPERTY FEES	
Real Estate Taxes	
Mortgage Interest or Rent	
HOA Fees	
Utilities	
Repairs and Maintenance	
Depreciation Expense	
Homeowners Insurance	
TOTAL:	

Have you depreciated any assets in the last year? ☐ YES ☐ NO
- If 'YES" attach your deprecation schedules.

The information provided above is true and accurate to the best of my knowledge.

_____

NAME *(SIGNATURE WILL BE RECORDED IN DOCU-SIGN)*

_____

TITLE

DUPLICATE THIS FORM FOR EACH PROPERTY.

Conclusion

Our goal with this book was to give you a basic understanding of home-based businesses, all of the benefits they
have to offer, and how you can get started today. Starting
a business doesn't happen without effort—money doesn't
start falling from the sky when you start a home-based
business—but that effort sure does make it easier to keep
your money in your own pockets!

If you'd like to learn more about how to equip yourself
with the necessary knowledge about navigating the world
of taxes for your home-based business, check out our
other book, *More Relaxing Less Taxing for Network Marketers due out fall of 2020*. We're also here to help in any
way we can, and between the two of us, we have a lot of

bases covered. Courtney's tax strategy business, Outside the Box Business Solutions, otbtax.com is a full-service accounting firm. She'd be happy to have a consultation with you to review your taxes and explore what's possible. If you're looking for support on achieving greater success in your business, Rob's private community on Facebook, Top Learners Club, is a great place to get started, and also where you can receive individual coaching from him. To connect with Rob go to his website robertamcfadden. com and check it out or send him and email directly at rob@robertamcfadden.com.

We're fueled by dreams and passions, by giving back and making connections, and by seeing people live into their fullest potential and finally feeling proud of their lives. We hope this book gives you the boost you need to tap into the vast rewards of owning your own home-based business. And there's no better time to start taking action than today!

We're fueled by dreams and passions, by giving back and making connections, and by seeing people live into their fullest potential and finally feeling proud of their lives.

Endnotes

1. Warren Buffett Says: "'Always Have 2 Sources of Income' – Why and How to Do It." *Warren Buffett,* Wikiquote, 21 Oct. 2018, 15:32, en.wikiquote.org/wiki/Warren_Buffett.

2. Botkin, Sanford C., *Lower Your Taxes—Big Time!: Wealth-Building, Tax Reduction Secrets from an IRS Insider,* 2016–2017 edition (McGraw-Hill Education, 2017).

3. Ibid. Information in this book is also taken from these sources: Botkin, Sanford C., *Seven Simple Ways to Legally Avoid Paying Taxes* (Taxbot LLC, 2018). Kiyosaki, Robert T., *Rich Dads Retire Young, Retire Rich: How to Get Rich Quickly and Stay Rich Forever* (Warner Books, 2012).

4. Kohler, Mark J., *What Your CPA Isn't Telling You: Life-Changing Tax Strategies* (Entrepreneur Media Inc., 2011). "10 Commonly Overlooked Tax Breaks for the Self-Employed," Quickbooks, 2018, quickbooks.intuit.com/r/taxes/10-commonly-overlooked-tax-breaks-for-the-selfemployed/.

A great deal of information in this book is taken from the Internal Revenue Code. Various sections cited. These are carefully listed throughout.

About the Authors

COURTNEY EPPS is the wife of Brandon Epps and the proud mother of six children. The family lives in Greenville, South Carolina. She has more than eighteen years of experience in the accounting and finance industry. She is a Fractional CFO to more than a dozen small- to medium-sized companies and owns a full-service accounting firm, Outside the Box Business Solutions, LLC. She has owned her business for seventeen years. Her experience is in public and cost accounting, providing clients with tax preparation, tax planning, income tax accounting, and consulting services to better run a business. With years of experience, she has developed advanced technical skills in a wide variety of tax and accounting areas and has served clients from start-up businesses to multi-million-dollar companies. Courtney has worked with companies that span a range of industries and sizes. She has developed a broad expertise of industries including trucking, doctor's offices, real estate, construction, convention companies, and others, as well as home-based and network marketing businesses.

ROBERT A. MCFADDEN has been married to his wife Tamara for 25 years. They have nine kids which include some biological, some adopted, and currently one beautiful daughter-in-law. He and his family live in New Canaan, Connecticut. Robert has a bachelor's degree from Utah State University in Sales and Marketing and a master's degree from Johns Hopkins University. Robert has been a serial entrepreneur for most of his life. The start of his entrepreneurial journey is detailed in his next book, *Theory of Optimism*. You can pre-order a copy at theoryofoptimism.com. It is due out fall of 2020. Much of Robert's business focus has been split between two areas, real estate and relationship marketing. Both of these pursuits have an equal hold on his heart for largely the same reasons: (1) the thrill of building something from scratch, and (2) residual income. To conceive of something and then create it to match your original vision is truly inspiring, and to be paid for that effort after the end goal has been reached makes the effort all the more worth it. Robert has built a thriving coaching and consulting business that helps individuals and businesses maximize their potential in all areas of business. Robert's consulting clients range from the brand-new entrepreneur just starting out to multi-billion-dollar companies. Robert has developed a private community of coaching clients online as well under the name Top LEarners Club, where Learners are Earners. You can check it out on his website, robertamcfadden.com. If you feel like you lack a piece to your puzzle and could benefit from a community of like-minded entrepreneurs, or even some private coaching, inquire at robertamcfadden.com.

Text LEVEL UP to 917-982-2868 to get added to Robert's contacts and hear firsthand about all upcoming events happening. Contact Rob directly at rob@robertamcfadden.com to connect with him about his private coaching community, booking him for a speaking engagement, if you're interested in going on an international service trip or learning more about the charities he supports – ALL GOOD REASONS TO REACH OUT!

ARE YOU STUCK
trying to grow your Relationship Marketing
—— BUSINESS? ——

Time to LEARN, Time to EARN!

Join the **Top LEarners Club** - *Where Learners are Earners*

Online at **RobertAMcFadden.com**, or

Text - **"Level Up"** to **917-982-2868** or

Email - **join@thesidehustle.pro**

ACCORDING TO FORBES:
"MORE THAN 90% OF BUSINESS OWNERS AND ENTREPRENEURS ARE OVERPAYING IN TAXES!"

DON'T ALLOW THE IRS
TO ROB YOU OF YOUR
HARD-EARNED MONEY!

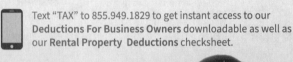

Text "TAX" to 855.949.1829 to get instant access to our **Deductions For Business Owners** downloadable as well as our **Rental Property Deductions** checksheet.

*WE WANT YOU TO BE ABLE TO FIND **US** SO THAT WE CAN HELP FIND **YOU** MONEY!*

Schedule your Tax Strategy Session with us today at:
WhatsYourPlanB.YouCanBook.Me

Courtney Epps
FRACTIONAL CFO
TAX STRATEGIST
AUTHOR

PHONE: 855.949.1829
EMAIL: info@otbtax.com
WEB: otbtax.com
SOCIAL: @otbtax

Be sure to subscribe to OTB Tax YouTube Channel and request to join our Facebook Group:

More Relaxing Less Taxing Monthly!

My suggestion is to find a home-based business or direct sales company in which you are passionate about their products or services and share those products with friends and family, allowing you to attempt to earn an income per the IRS. Not only could you make an extra stream of income, you can also decrease your tax burden at the same time and help people along the way. Decreasing taxes is truly the fastest way to wealth. I hope this has shown you how owning a home-based business can drastically alter your financial situation, both in income and tax relief with little time commitment.

What is your Plan B? I suggest that you find one today so that you can truly have a more relaxing and less taxing life. Now get back with the person that shared this with you and go out and help more, have more, do more, save more, and give more.

CRACK YOUR PERSONALITY
CODE
IN 90 SECONDS
———————— OR LESS

CODE BREAKER TECHNOLOGIES

"THE BANKCODE ASSESSMENT™ IS A QUICK, RELIABLE, AND VALID MEASURE OF PERSONALITIES THAT PREDICTS BUYING BEHAVIOR AND INCREASES YOUR PROBABILITY OF CLOSING THE SALE."

- DR. RYAN HOWELL
SR. DATA ANALYST | CODEBREAKER ANALYTICS

CRACK YOUR CODE NOW AND RECEIVE YOUR FREE BANKCODE REPORT!

CRACKMYCODE.COM /COURTNEY